THE HARLEM RENAISSANCE

DRAMA OF AFRICAN-AMERICAN HISTORY

THE HARLEM RENAISSANCE

by DOLORES JOHNSON with VIRGINIA SCHOMP

Marshall Cavendish
Benchmark
New York

ACKNOWLEDGMENTS

The authors and publisher are grateful to Jill Watts, professor of history at California State University, San Marcos, for her perceptive comments on the manuscript, and to the late Richard Newman, civil rights advocate, author, and senior research officer at the W. E. B. DuBois Institute at Harvard University, for his excellent work in formulating the series.

——— A NOTE ON LANGUAGE ———

In order to preserve the character and historical accuracy of the quoted material appearing in this book, we have not corrected or modernized spellings, capitalization, punctuation, or grammar. We have retained the "dialect spelling" that was sometimes used by white writers in an attempt to reproduce the way some black southerners spoke. You will occasionally come across outdated or offensive words, such as *colored*, *Negro*, and *nigger*, which were often used by both white and black Americans in the early twentieth century.

EDITOR: JOYCE STANTON   PUBLISHER: MICHELLE BISSON
ART DIRECTOR: ANAHID HAMPARIAN   SERIES DESIGNER: MICHAEL NELSON

MARSHALL CAVENDISH BENCHMARK 99 WHITE PLAINS ROAD TARRYTOWN, NEW YORK 10591-9001 www.marshallcavendish.us Text copyright © 2008 Dolores Johnson All rights reserved. No part of this book may be reproduced or utilized in any form or by any means electronic or mechanical including photocopying, recording, or by any information storage and retrieval system, without permission from the copyright holders. All Internet sites were available and accurate when this book was sent to press. LIBRARY OF CONGRESS CATALOGING-IN-PUBLICATION DATA: Johnson, Dolores, 1949- The Harlem Renaissance / by Dolores Johnson with Virginia Schomp. p. cm. Summary: "Covers a period of great creativity in the African-American community, when art, literature, music, and political commentary flourished; centered in Harlem, the era reached its peak in the 1920s and early 1930s"—Provided by publisher. Includes bibliographical references and index. ISBN 978-0-7614-2641-7 1. African Americans—Intellectual life—20th century—Juvenile literature. 2. Harlem Renaissance--Juvenile literature. 3. African American arts—20th century—Juvenile literature. 4. African Americans—History—1877-1964—Juvenile literature. 5. Harlem (New York, N.Y.)—Intellectual life—20th century—Juvenile literature. 6. African Americans—New York (State)—New York—Intellectual life--20th century—Juvenile literature. 7. African American arts—New York (State)—New York--History—20th century—Juvenile literature. 8. New York (N.Y.)—Intellectual life—20th century—Juvenile literature. I. Schomp, Virginia. II. Title. E185.6.J666 2008 305.896'073—dc22 2007034691

Illustrations assembled by Rose Corbett Gordon and Alexandra H. C. Gordon, Art Editors of Mystic CT, from the following sources: Cover: Time & Life Pictures/Getty Images Back cover: Michael Ochs Archives/Getty Images Pages i, 20, 54, 60, 61: Smithsonian American Art Museum, Washington, DC/Art Resource, NY; pages ii, 29: Underwood & Underwood/Corbis; page 6: Tate Gallery, London/Art Resource, NY; page 8: National Portrait Gallery, Smithsonian Institution/Art Resource, NY; pages 10, 57, 69: Schomburg Center/Art Resource, NY; pages 12, 23, 53 top & bottom, 63, 72: Corbis; pages 13, 19, 24, 30, 38, 46: Bettmann/Corbis; pages 15, 35: Private Collection/ Peter Newark American Pictures/ The Bridgeman Art Library; page 17: The Philips Collection, Washington, D.C. ©2007 The Jacob and Gwendolyn Lawrence Foundation, Seattle/ Artists Rights Society (ARS), New York; pages 22, 42, 48 top, 48 bottom, 50, 56, 66: Yale Collection of American Literature, Beinecke Rare Book & Manuscript Library; pages 27, 34, 36: Hulton Archive/Getty Images; page 33 top: Lebrecht Music & Arts/The Image Works; page 33 bottom: John Springer Collection, Corbis; page 39: The Jacob and Gwendolyn Lawrence Foundation / Art Resource, NY; pages 40, 41: Photofest; page 45: Schomburg Center for Research on Black Culture/The New York Public Library ©Topham/The Image Works; page 51: Howard University; page 58: Courtesy of Renate Reiss; page 59: The Barnes Foundation, Merion, Pennsylvania/ The Bridgeman Art Library; page 62: Photographs and Prints Division, Schomburg Center for Research in Black Culture, The New York Public Library, Astor, Lenox and Tilden Foundations; page 64: Lucien Aigner/Corbis.

"The Negro Speaks of Rivers," copyright ©1994 by The Estate of Langston Hughes, from THE COLLECTED POEMS OF LANGSTON HUGHES by Langston Hughes. Used by permission of Alfred A. Knopf, a division of Random House, Inc.

Printed in China
1 3 5 6 4 2

Front cover: The Cotton Club in Harlem, 1937
Back cover: Blues singer Gertrude "Ma" Rainey and her Georgia Jazz Band
Half-title page: *Children at the Ice Cream Stand* by William H. Johnson, painted between 1939 and 1942
Title page: A stroll along Harlem's Lenox Avenue, around 1929

CONTENTS

INTRODUCTION

The Harlem Renaissance is the seventh book in the series Drama of African-American History. Earlier books in this series have traced the journey of African Americans from slavery to emancipation to the beginnings of the "Jim Crow" system around the end of the nineteenth century. Now we will explore the extraordinary era known as the Harlem Renaissance.

The Harlem Renaissance was a period of tremendous creativity in the African-American community. This flowering of art, literature, music, and political commentary reached its peak in the 1920s and early 1930s, although its roots can be traced all the way back to the end of the Civil War. The Renaissance was centered in the Harlem section of New York City. During the 1920s and early 1930s, Harlem was the place to be for talented black intellectuals, writers, artists, and performers. Its teeming streets and lively nightclubs attracted and nurtured a new generation of African Americans, brimming with fresh ideas and inventive new ways to express them. Many of their ideas and innovations would radiate beyond the Harlem community and endure long after the Renaissance ended.

Of course black people had been a part of American life and culture long before the Harlem Renaissance. Over the centuries

Opposite: Harlem, by British artist Edward Burra, captured the "cool," flashy, sophisticated style of New York's vibrant black neighborhood.

Actor and civil rights activist Paul Robeson in 1924. This portrait was created by Winold Reiss, a German-born artist known for his depictions of Native Americans and African Americans.

there had been a number of African Americans who overcame the many obstacles against their race and distinguished themselves as writers, artists, and musicians. The early years of the twentieth century had produced several notable black writers, including poet Paul Laurence Dunbar and novelist Charles Waddell Chesnutt. Before the Renaissance, however, there had never been such a profusion of African-American culture, with so many men and women generating so much creative work with such energy, optimism, and enthusiasm.

History books often describe the Harlem Renaissance as a "cultural movement." That phrase usually refers to an organized group of people working together for a common goal. While the leaders of the Renaissance did share some of the same goals, they did not always agree on the many complex issues facing their race. They argued long and loud over the role of art and artists in the black community. They produced work in many different forms and styles, including some that had never been seen before. What united all these gifted individuals was their two-part mission: first, to create wonderful art and literature and, second, to celebrate the history, achievements, and unlimited potential of black Americans.

Cheering crowds celebrate the return of the famous World War I regiment known as the Harlem Hell Fighters.

Chapter 1

ROOTS OF THE HARLEM RENAISSANCE

ON A CHILLY MORNING IN FEBRUARY 1919, THE men of the 369th Infantry Regiment marched up New York's Fifth Avenue. Cheering crowds lined the streets. The brave black soldiers had won glory fighting German forces in World War I. Their spirit and daring had earned them an admiring nickname from America's French allies: the Hell Fighters. France had also honored the black troops with the Croix de Guerre, its highest decoration for courage in action.

Almost as famous as the fighting men of the 369th was the regiment's sixty-piece jazz band, commanded by James Reese Europe. The band played stirring military music for the victory march through Manhattan. As the soldiers reached the uptown neighborhood of Harlem, however, the music suddenly changed. The band broke into the jazz hit "Here Comes My Daddy Now," and the crowds roared their approval. Black men, women, and children poured into the streets to welcome their returning heroes. "For the final mile or more of our parade," recalled one black enlisted man, "about every fourth soldier of the ranks had a girl upon his arm—and we marched through Harlem singing and laughing."

"WE RETURN FIGHTING"

Historians disagree over exactly when the Harlem Renaissance began. For many, it was the day the men of the 369th Infantry Regiment made their triumphant return to Harlem. Their overseas experiences had given the black soldiers pride, confidence, and a new sense of their place in the world. Those qualities would inspire all African Americans in the continuing battle against racial injustice.

The 1,300 Hell Fighters were just a small part of the nearly 400,000 African Americans who served in World War I. America had gone to war pledging to make the world "safe for democracy." Patriotic black men had joined the fight even though democracy seemed a distant dream in their own homeland. Many black leaders hoped that the loyalty and sacrifices of black soldiers would persuade whites to support the American ideals of liberty and justice for all.

Those hopes soon faded. Black soldiers faced discrimination and hostility both within the army and in the small towns surrounding their training camps. They served in all-black units, commanded mainly by

The Hell Fighters received 171 individual citations for bravery. These soldiers were awarded France's prestigious Croix de Guerre.

THE HARLEM RENAISSANCE

white officers. The great majority of black troops were restricted to manual labor. Only four regiments, including the 369th Infantry, were given a chance to prove themselves in combat. Serving under French leadership, those troops were treated as equals. All four regiments distinguished themselves in battle.

No matter how capable and courageous black soldiers proved themselves, they returned home to racism and discrimination. During the late 1800s, the Jim Crow system had taken root across the United States, especially in the South. This complex set of laws and practices stripped blacks of their rights and imposed segregation in practically every area of public life.

Racist white Americans enforced the Jim Crow restrictions through intimidation and violence. During the World War I years, nearly one hundred African Americans were murdered by white lynch mobs in the South. Racial violence also rocked northern cities. In fact, one of the worst race riots the country

A man moves his belongings to safety under police protection during the Chicago race riot of 1919.

had ever seen took place in East St. Louis, Illinois. White laborers in East St. Louis resented the employment of blacks in the city's factories. In July 1917 their anger and racial hatred erupted into three days of rioting. White mobs set the black section of the city in flames and killed hundreds of black men, women, and children.

Following the East St. Louis riot, black leaders organized a Silent Protest Parade in New York City. Dressed in mourning

clothes, thousands of African Americans marched silently down Fifth Avenue to the beat of muffled drums. Signs and banners voiced their outrage:

GIVE US A CHANCE TO LIVE.

YOUR HANDS ARE FULL OF BLOOD.

MR. PRESIDENT, WHY NOT MAKE AMERICA SAFE FOR DEMOCRACY?

One of the organizers of the Silent Protest Parade was W. E. B. DuBois (pronounced doo-BOYCE).* As a cofounder and director of the National Association for the Advancement of Colored People (NAACP), DuBois had urged blacks to support their country in World War I. Outraged by the racial attacks that continued even as black soldiers trained for war, he helped lead the silent protesters down Fifth Avenue. Two years later, as the Hell Fighters marched triumphantly up that same avenue, DuBois would issue a stirring new call to action:

We return.

We return from fighting.

We return fighting.

Make way for Democracy! We saved it in France, and by the Great Jehovah, we will save it in the United States of America, or know the reason why.

THE GREAT MIGRATION

The rising tide of violence in northern cities following World War I was partly the result of a massive change in America's

*For more on W. E. B. DuBois, see volume 6 in this series, *The Rise of Jim Crow.*

THE RED SUMMER

James Weldon Johnson, one of the leaders of the Harlem Renaissance, called the second half of 1919 the Red Summer. During that bloody period, an epidemic of racial violence swept the United States. There were race riots in at least twenty-five cities. More than seventy blacks, including several veterans in uniform, were murdered by lynch mobs. Meanwhile, the Ku Klux Klan, a southern white terrorist group that had declined in the 1870s, surged to new life as a nationwide organization with hundreds of thousands of members.

A Ku Klux Klan "family" snapshot from around 1930. Parents often pass on their prejudices.

Black Americans had always been the target of white intimidation and violence. What was new in the post–World War I years was the way they responded to the attacks. No longer willing to wait and hope for protection from local authorities or the federal government, many African Americans armed themselves and fought back. During a four-day riot in Washington, D.C., hundreds of whites swarmed the streets, beating or shooting every black man, woman, and child they found. When the rioters tried to enter a black neighborhood, however, they were met by a crowd of armed black men. More than one hundred people were wounded or killed before federal troops restored order.

In his poem "If We Must Die," Claude McKay expressed the defiant attitude of a new generation of African Americans determined to take up arms in their country's growing race war.

> If we must die, O let us nobly die,
> So that our precious blood may not be shed
> In vain; then even the monsters we defy
> Shall be constrained to honor us though dead!

racial landscape. In 1910, 90 percent of African Americans still lived in the South, mostly in rural areas. Around 1915 vast numbers of these southern blacks began to migrate to the North. By the time the Great Migration slowed down in 1930, about two million southern black men, women, and children had resettled in northern industrial centers, including Chicago, Detroit, Pittsburgh, Cleveland, and New York City.

Many blacks migrated to escape the relentless racism, injustice, and brutality in the South. Letters sent home by friends and family members who had already gone north added fuel to the "migration fever." One black man wrote from Philadelphia, telling a friend back home in "the good old South" that he no longer had to

> mister every little white boy comes along I havent heard a white man call a colored a nigger . . . since I been in the state of Pa. I can ride in the electric street and steam cars any where I get a seat . . . and if you are first in a place here shoping you dont have to wait until the white folks get thro tradeing. . . . I am praying that God may give every well wisher a chance to be a man regardless of his color.

Southern blacks also moved to the North seeking greater economic security. During 1915 and 1916, southern farms were ravaged by drought, floods, and the boll weevil, a tiny pest that gobbled its way through cotton crops. At the same time, the outbreak of war in Europe halted the flow of foreign workers to the United States. Northern companies, booming with wartime orders, were desperate for laborers. They placed ads in south-

ern newspapers, offering good jobs at good wages. Railroad companies, shipyards, mines, and factories sent labor agents to recruit southern black workers. Some agents gave out free train passes to prospective employees. Others "loaned" the tickets, with the costs to be deducted from future wages.

For most black migrants, there was no free ride. Some families sold all their possessions to finance the long, expensive journey north. Others made the trip in stages, stopping to work in cities along the way. The Harlem Renaissance painter Jacob Lawrence recalled spending most of his childhood traveling. His family "was moving up the coast, as many families were during that migration." They stopped for long stretches in cities including Atlantic City, New Jersey; Easton, Pennsylva-

Jacob Lawrence told the story of the Great Migration in a series of sixty paintings, beginning with this image of a crowded southern railway station.

nia; and Philadelphia. When Jacob was thirteen, they finally reached their destination. It was a place of bright lights and excitement, of music and color, a place "full of life, full of vitality, full of energy." It was Harlem.

The Capital of Black America

In 1900 the section of northern Manhattan known as Harlem was a white upper-class neighborhood of fine homes and apartment buildings. Developers had sunk a fortune into new construction in Harlem, hoping to strike it rich when subway lines reached the neighborhood. Subway construction had been delayed, however. Many of the buildings stood empty, and developers were getting desperate.

Then a young African-American real estate agent named Philip A. Payton came up with a solution to their problems. Payton knew that many African Americans were living in crowded, crime-ridden slums scattered throughout New York City. Middle-class black families would gladly pay inflated rents to live on the broad tree-lined avenues of Harlem. The realtor struck a deal with one of the white apartment owners. He would manage the man's building, renting the vacant apartments to "respectable" black families for five dollars a month more than white tenants.

The arrangement was so successful that Payton was soon managing several buildings. Other black men and women began to open their own real estate firms in Harlem. At first, white residents protested the "Negro invasion." A local newspaper urged whites to "wake up and get busy before it is too late to repel the black hordes." Despite the objections, white property owners continued to rent and sell to blacks. White residents

began to move out of Harlem. Block by block, year by year, the black section of the neighborhood expanded. By 1914, *The Outlook* magazine reported that Harlem had become "a Negro city in New York."

By the 1930s, Harlem was America's largest black "city within a city."

Over the next two decades, the Great Migration would continue to bring tens of thousands of southern black migrants to Harlem. The small, crowded New York neighborhood would become the largest black community in the United States. The growing African-American population also attracted many of the country's leading black intellectuals and writers. Under their guidance Harlem would be transformed into the political and cultural capital of black America.

Harlem Renaissance painter William H. Johnson captured the richness of African-American culture in bold, brightly colored paintings.

Chapter 2

A New Identity

HARLEM GREW UP AT AN EXCITING TIME IN African-American history. In the past most African Americans had followed a policy of "accommodation." They had tried to adapt to prejudice and injustice, hoping to advance their race through patience, hard work, and peaceful cooperation with their white oppressors. Now they were demanding an end to oppression. They were rejecting the old images imposed on them by whites, which portrayed all black people as lazy, ignorant, and inferior. In place of those stereotypes, African Americans were working to create a new identity for themselves as a people. That new black consciousness emphasized racial pride, self-respect, and self-determination.

A small group of black intellectuals helped translate the dynamic spirit of the early 1920s into what would become known as the New Negro Movement or Harlem Renaissance.

These leaders believed that art could be used as a potent weapon against white supremacy. They issued a call for promising young black writers and artists to come to Harlem. They encouraged these rising stars to create works celebrating African-American culture and achievements. By showing the world their intelligence, talents, and contributions, black men and women would prove themselves "worthy" of their full rights as American citizens.

The cover for this issue of the NAACP magazine *The Crisis* was created by Harlem Renaissance artist Aaron Douglas.

THE "FOUNDING FATHERS"

One of the most brilliant promoters of the Harlem Renaissance was W. E. B. DuBois. Decades earlier, DuBois had emerged as a leading opponent of accommodationism and a fierce champion of civil rights. As editor of the NAACP magazine *The Crisis*, he demanded full and immediate equality for blacks. He also challenged what he called the "Talented Tenth"—the most intelligent and accomplished African Americans—to work for the advancement of the entire race. In 1920 DuBois inspired many young black writers and artists with his call for a "renaissance of American Negro literature. . . . The material about us in the strange, heart-rending race tangle is rich beyond dream and only we can tell the tale and sing the song from the heart."

James Weldon Johnson was a shining example of DuBois's Talented Tenth. By the time Johnson moved to Harlem in 1914, he had already excelled in at least seven different careers: teacher, poet, novelist, songwriter, newspaper editor, lawyer, and diplomat. Now he was ready to help lead the struggle against racial injustice. Johnson waged his battle on two fronts.

"LIFT EVERY VOICE AND SING"

James Weldon Johnson was a true "Renaissance man" (a term that means a person with many different interests and talents). How appropriate that he should become one of the leaders of the Harlem Renaissance! Johnson's many talents included songwriting. In 1900 he wrote the lyrics for "Lift Every Voice and Sing." His brother, J. Rosamond Johnson, composed the music. Here are the first two stanzas from their popular hymn, which is often called the "black national anthem."

Lift ev'ry voice and sing,
Till earth and heaven ring,
Ring with the harmonies of Liberty;
Let our rejoicing rise
High as the list'ning skies,
Let it resound loud as the rolling sea.

Sing a song full of the faith that the
    dark past has taught us,
Sing a song full of the hope that the
    present has brought us;
Facing the rising sun of our new day
    begun,
*Let us march on till victory is won.**

*You can read the full text of James Weldon Johnson's "Lift Every Voice and Sing" online at http://www.poets.org/viewmedia.php/prmMID/15588

Above: Writer, educator, and civil rights leader James Weldon Johnson

As the first black executive secretary of the NAACP, he worked with W. E. B. DuBois in the fight for civil rights. As a scholar, he gave young black writers, artists, and musicians the keys to their cultural heritage. Johnson made a lengthy study of black music and literature, then published the first anthologies of traditional African-American poetry and spirituals. He urged the new generation of black artists to build on these foundations of their culture. "The world does not know that a people is great," he wrote, "until that people produces great literature and art."

Another important elder statesman of the Harlem Renaissance was Alain Locke. A graduate of Harvard University, Locke became the first African American to win a Rhodes Scholarship to Oxford University in England. As a professor at Howard University, one of America's leading black colleges, he encouraged students to explore black culture alongside the great civilizations of the world. He also challenged young writers and artists to find inspiration in their African and African-American roots.

Harlem, the cultural capital of black America, on a summer day in 1935

In 1925 Locke published *The New Negro*, an anthology of essays, stories, and poems by young black writers. The term "New Negro" was often used to describe the proud, spirited younger generation of African Americans. These New Negroes, wrote Locke, were freeing themselves from the old racist stereotypes and rediscovering their own unique culture. Their vision of opportunity and advancement would usher in a "spiritual Coming of Age" for all African Americans. And the place where that revolution would take place was Harlem, the thriving metropolis where the "pulse of the Negro world [had] begun to beat."

A Coming Out Party

W. E. B. DuBois, James Weldon Johnson, and Alain Locke were larger-than-life personalities. In contrast, Charles S. Johnson liked to call himself a "sidelines activist." Working behind the scenes, this tireless promoter may have done more than any other leader to make the Harlem Renaissance possible.

Johnson was a social scientist who had devoted himself to studying race relations and racial violence. His research had convinced him that the best way for African Americans to combat racism and take their rightful place in American society was through literature. In the early 1920s, he found just the tool to help make that dream a reality. Moving to New York City, Johnson became the editor of *Opportunity*, a monthly journal published by the Urban League, a leading civil rights organization.

From his office in Harlem, Charles Johnson sought out unknown black writers from across the United States. He was especially interested in young men and women whose work explored the black experience in America. Johnson invited these budding talents to New York, where he found them free meals and a couch to sleep on while they were getting established. He edited their writings and published their best works in the pages of *Opportunity*. He also organized a series of literary contests and awards banquets to introduce these rising stars to the white publishing world.

Johnson called the first of his literary get-togethers a "coming out party" for the Harlem Renaissance. In March 1924 he organized a dinner at the Civic Club, one of New York's few integrated restaurants. The guest list included influential white publishers and magazine editors, distinguished white authors, and promising young black writers. Among the speakers were noted black intellectuals such as W. E. B. DuBois, Alain Locke, and James Weldon Johnson. "It was a most unusual affair," wrote Charles Johnson,

> a dinner meeting at the Civic Club at which all of the younger Negro writers . . . met and chatted with the passing generation . . . and with the literary personages of the city—about 100 guests and tremendously impressive speaking. . . . It served to stimulate a market for the new stuff which these young writers are turning out.

The Civic Club dinner opened up new avenues for black writers. Before 1924 the "New Negroes" had published mainly in small black-owned journals. Now white publishers began to seek out their poems, novels, short stories, and essays. For the first time, African Americans were reaching a national audience of both black and white readers.

The Rise and Fall of Marcus Garvey

In the spring of 1916, black labor leader A. Philip Randolph gave a speech before a crowd in Harlem. At the conclusion Randolph announced that a young man from Jamaica had asked to say a few words. The speaker was Marcus Garvey. One member of the audience would later describe him as "a little sawed-off, hammered down black man, with determination written all over his face, and

A. PHILIP RANDOLPH AND THE LABOR MOVEMENT

Asa Philip Randolph, who helped introduce Marcus Garvey to Harlem, was a leading intellectual and a champion of the black working class. Randolph believed that the best way to fight racial oppression was to organize black labor. In his magazine, *The Messenger*, he argued that

> the Negro must engage in direct action. He is forced to do this by the Government. When the whites speak of direct action, they are told to use their political power. But with the Negro it is different. He has no political power. Therefore the only recourse the Negro has is industrial action.

In 1925 A. Philip Randolph founded the Brotherhood of Sleeping Car Porters and Maids. The union represented thousands of African-American porters and maids working for the Pullman Company, operator of sleeping and dining cars for the nation's railroads. Over the next twelve years, Randolph led union members in their battle for better working conditions. He succeeded in winning higher wages as well as passage of the Railway Labor Act, which protected the organizing rights of Pullman workers. In 1935 the Brotherhood of Sleeping Car Porters would become the first black organization to join the nation's largest union alliance, the American Federation of Labor (AFL).

Above: A Pullman porter surveys a line of shoes left out for polishing in a railroad sleeping car.

an engaging smile that . . . compelled you to listen to his story."

Marcus Garvey had quite a story to tell. Two years earlier, in his native Jamaica, he had founded the Universal Negro Improvement Association (UNIA). The organization was rooted in pan-Africanism, the idea that people of African descent all over the world should unite to fight their common enemies, including oppression and racism. Garvey had come to the United States to drum up members for the UNIA. He urged black Americans to take pride in their racial heritage. He warned them that they would never achieve equality within America's racist society. Instead of pursuing that impossible goal, they should work to become self-sufficient by establishing their own independent businesses and institutions. The UNIA also proposed that black Americans return to their African homeland and build a separate nation, where they could live free of white domination. "Up you mighty race," he cried out to audiences. "Let us work toward the one glorious end [goal] of a free, redeemed and mighty nation."

Marcus Garvey's message stirred many African Americans, especially the masses of poor blacks living in overcrowded city slums. By 1920, the UNIA had hundreds of thousands of followers. That summer Garvey organized the first International Convention of the Negro Peoples of the World. More than 20,000 delegates from dozens of UNIA branches met in New York City to make plans for a future "Negro nation." Following the convention, crowds cheered as the flamboyant "provisional president" of that nation rode through Harlem, followed by hosts of his uniformed soldiers. One bystander watched spellbound as "thousands of Garvey legionnaires, resplendent in their uniforms marched by. When Garvey rode by in his plumed hat, I got an emotional lift, which swept me above the

THE HARLEM RENAISSANCE

poverty and the prejudice by which my life was limited."

Along with his admirers, Garvey had many critics. More moderate black leaders denounced him as an impractical fool. His separationist policies went against the main goal of organizations such as the NAACP: equal rights for African Americans *within* American society. W. E. B. DuBois, one of Garvey's harshest critics, called him "without doubt, the most dangerous threat to the Negro race in America and in the world."

In the end, however, it was not Marcus Garvey's critics but his business ventures that sank his remarkable career. In 1919 the controversial leader had launched his most ambitious project: the Black Star Line. This steamship company was intended to carry on commerce for black businesses and eventually transport black Americans back to Africa. Garvey raised ten million dollars selling shares in his Black Star Line. The first ship he bought turned out to be a worthless, overpriced tub. Further mismanagement soon left the company bankrupt. When Garvey sent out letters seeking additional funds, he was arrested for mail fraud. After two years in prison, he was deported back to Jamaica.

Marcus Garvey wears a splendid uniform and ostrich-plumed hat, designed to remind African Americans of their proud heritage.

Deprived of its popular president, the UNIA faded away. Many critics dismissed the organization's dramatic appeal as a fad. But in his time, Marcus Garvey had assembled the largest mass movement in African-American history. His message of racial pride and unity would inspire generations to come. Decades after Garvey's death, militant civil rights leader Malcolm X would proclaim, "Every time you see another nation on the African continent become independent, you know that Marcus Garvey is alive!"

Bessie Smith, "Empress of the Blues," sang about the hopes and heartaches of a new generation of African Americans.

Chapter 3

The Music of the Renaissance

IT WAS THE "ROARING TWENTIES." WORLD WAR
I was over, and the U.S. economy was booming. New inventions
and technologies were changing the way Americans worked and
lived. Small towns were shrinking, while cities grew by leaps and
bounds. In the face of all these changes, conservative Americans
longed for the "good old days" and favored traditional values.
Meanwhile, members of the younger generation were experimenting with new ideas, values, fashions, and fads.

Nowhere was the excitement of this colorful decade more evi-
dent than in Harlem. Thanks to the efforts of W. E. B. DuBois,
James Weldon Johnson, Alain Locke, Charles S. Johnson, and
other black leaders, the teeming New York neighborhood had
become a magnet for creative young African Americans. These
"New Negroes" were eagerly exploring and celebrating their cultural heritage. Meanwhile, "ordinary" people reveled in their

community's proud, vibrant, optimistic atmosphere.

Even white America caught "Harlemania." For fashionable young white men and women, the thriving uptown neighborhood was the place to go to enjoy the latest music and other forms of entertainment. The Harlem Renaissance was transforming not only African-American identity but the culture of America itself.

THE BLUES AND THE BEAT

Much of the character and spirit of the Harlem Renaissance came from music. African-American folk music reached back hundreds of years, to the early slave songs and spirituals. Black Americans built on that cultural heritage to create three brand-new music forms: ragtime, the blues, and jazz.

Ragtime first emerged in black communities around the end of the 1800s, a few decades before the Harlem Renaissance reached its peak. This lively music form blended traditional African-American rhythms and harmonies with European classical music. Its name came from its "ragged," or syncopated, rhythms. Syncopation puts the musical accents in unexpected places, off the beat, giving the music a lively, jaunty sound.

The "King of Ragtime" was the African-American composer and pianist Scott Joplin. Joplin's most famous composition was the wildly popular "Maple Leaf Rag," published in 1899.* On the eve of the Harlem Renaissance, Joplin moved to New York City. There he composed the first black grand opera, *Treemonisha*. The ragtime opera was a flop in its time. Sixty-five years later, long after the composer's death, it would win Joplin a special Pulitzer Prize.

*You can listen to an old piano-roll recording of Scott Joplin playing his "Maple Leaf Rag" at http://music.minnesota.publicradio.org/features/9905_ragtime/index.shtml

The blues grew out of traditional slave laments and work songs. These mournful melodies were first sung by slaves laboring in southern plantation fields. The blues followed the musical pattern of the old songs, adding lyrics that expressed the heartache of being broke, homesick, lonely, or longing for a lost love. The sad new songs were often sung in lively rhythms, with strength and laughter beneath the sorrow.

The most famous blues singers were African-American women. Gertrude "Ma" Rainey, often called the "Mother of the Blues," was a short, heavyset woman who loved to flaunt her furs and diamonds and flash her mouthful of glittering gold teeth. This bold and flamboyant woman became one of Harlem's brightest stars, belting out songs that were sometimes sad, sometimes naughty and humorous.

Ethel Waters came to New York in 1919 and established herself as one of Harlem's top entertainers. Her best-selling recordings of "Down Home Blues" and "Oh, Daddy" helped launch the country's first black-owned record label, Black Swan. Waters later built a second successful career as an actress in Broadway musicals and in movies.

Bessie Smith, the "Empress of the Blues," was one of the highest-paid black

Gertrude "Ma" Rainey introduced America to a new style of music known as the blues.

Ethel Waters stars in the 1929 movie musical *On with the Show.*

performers of her time. She recorded more than 150 songs and toured the country, thrilling audiences with her deep, expressive voice. Many of Smith's songs spoke of her awareness of herself as a strong, independent black woman. To poet Langston Hughes, her music was the essence of sadness "not softened with tears, but hardened with laughter, the absurd . . . laughter of a sadness without even a god to appeal to."

JAZZ COMES TO HARLEM

Around the start of the Harlem Renaissance, ragtime took a backseat to jazz. This new music craze combined elements of several different music forms, including ragtime, blues, traditional black spirituals, and brass-band music. Jazz had first emerged in New Orleans in the early 1900s. During the Great Migration, it had traveled along with southern black migrants to northern cities, including Chicago, Kansas City, and New York.

Duke Ellington is considered one of the greatest composers and musicians of the twentieth century.

Harlem fell in love with its driving beat, syncopated rhythms, and inventive melodies. Unlike more traditional music, jazz allowed performers to improvise, creating their own unique melodies and rhythms as they played.

One of the most celebrated jazz musicians was Edward Kennedy Ellington. As a young man, Ellington picked up the nickname "Duke" for his sophisticated manners and elegant style of dress. Duke Ellington began his career as a jazz pianist. He went on to become the leader of one of the first "big bands." The big bands performed carefully arranged jazz compositions, with several

THE HARLEM RENAISSANCE

players on each type of instrument.

The Duke Ellington Orchestra played dance music at the hottest nightclubs in Harlem. In later years it would tour nearly every country in the Western world. Ellington was also one of America's greatest composers. Over the course of six decades, he produced more than three thousand musical compositions, writing for stage productions, movies, ballet companies, and symphony orchestras. His complex jazz compositions featured rich, inventive harmonies as well as solos that reflected the special qualities of each instrument and musician. Ellington once said that he didn't try to write jazz. "All I do is write and play Negro folk music."

Harlem's other jazz giants included Fletcher Henderson and Louis Armstrong. Henderson formed the first big band in 1923. His ten-piece orchestra became the model imitated by nearly every other jazz band to come. Louis Armstrong moved from New Orleans to Harlem in 1924 to play in Henderson's band. His exciting and innovative trumpet solos made him an instant sensation. He also popularized a new kind of jazz singing called scat. In scat singing, performers use their voices like musical instruments, singing sounds or nonsense syllables instead of words. In later years, Louis Armstrong would become as famous for his gravelly singing voice as for his golden horn.

Louis Armstrong explained his passion for music this way: "My whole life, my whole soul, my whole spirit is to blow that horn."

HARLEM AFTER DARK
By day, Harlem's streets teemed with black workingmen and women, mothers and children,

Jazz bandleader Cab Calloway dances with a line of chorus girls at the famous Cotton Club.

pushcart peddlers, and the poor and homeless. After dark a whole new scene emerged. Black folks strolled to parties, dressed in their most stylish clothes. White folks from other parts of New York came to relax after a hard day at the office or an elegant evening at the theater. Like white novelist Max Ewing, these pleasure seekers saw Harlem as "the one place that is gay and delightful however dull and depressing the downtown regions may be. Nothing affects the vitality and the freshness of Harlem."

Most whites were drawn to the nightclubs on Harlem's "Jungle Alley," a stretch of 133rd Street where jazz bands blazed and blues singers crooned. The most famous of these hot spots was the Cotton Club. Here the elaborate floor shows featured a chorus line of long-legged dancers, who performed fast-paced routines while a big band played. Some of Harlem's most celebrated performers appeared at the Cotton Club, including the Duke Ellington Orchestra, trumpeter Louis Armstrong, blues singers Ethel Waters and Edith Wilson, and dancers Earl "Snakehips" Tucker and Bill "Bojangles" Robinson.

THE HARLEM RENAISSANCE

Like nearly all of Harlem's glamorous nightclubs, the Cotton Club was segregated. The musicians, singers, dancers, comedians, and waiters were all black. The customers were all white. White tourists liked the idea of "experiencing" black culture without actually having to mingle with blacks. The tropical decorations and "jungle" sounds, such as roaring and growling horn instruments, contributed to the club's "primitive" atmosphere.

The white people who flocked to Harlem thought that black residents enjoyed having them there. Many African Americans did agree that some good came from the mingling of "downtowners" and "uptowners," especially when the money spent by wealthy whites paid the salaries of black workers and performers. At the same time, Harlemites resented the prejudiced attitudes behind the white "invasion." According to poet Langston Hughes,

> Harlem Negroes did not like the Cotton Club and never appreciated its Jim Crow policy in the very heart of their dark community, nor did ordinary Negroes like the growing influx of whites toward Harlem after sundown, flooding the little cabarets and bars where formerly only colored people laughed and sang, and where now the strangers were given the best ringside tables to sit and stare at the [Negroes]—like amusing animals in a zoo.

The Cotton Club and Harlem's other popular nightclubs were fancy "speakeasies." This was the era of Prohibition. Manufacturing and selling alcohol were prohibited, but illegal or "bootleg" liquor flowed freely at the speakeasies.

Couples dance away the night at one of Harlem's many small, crowded speakeasies.

Some white patrons skipped the big nightclubs, preferring the more casual atmosphere at the hundreds of small, crowded speakeasies located in the side streets off Jungle Alley. Here adventurous whites mingled with the black customers who packed the tiny dance floors. Some speakeasies stayed open till dawn, swinging to the music of small jazz bands. Famous black performers often stopped by after the nightclubs closed. "The average musician in Harlem hated to go home those days," recalled drummer William "Sonny" Greer. "Someplace, somewhere 'cats' were jamming, and nobody wanted to miss anything."

FROM HARLEM TO BROADWAY

Before the Harlem Renaissance, musical theater was practically closed to blacks. A few African-American composers and performers, including J. Rosamond Johnson, Bob Cole,

RENT PARTIES

The great majority of Harlem's black residents never saw the inside of a nightclub or speakeasy. Ordinary working people—cooks, maids, laundresses, barbers, cabdrivers, elevator operators, laborers—did not have the time or money to spend their nights drinking "bootleg liquor" in crowded nightspots. Instead, most Harlemites got their share of music and dancing at the informal gatherings known as rent parties.

The rents in Harlem were high. Black apartment dwellers in the neighborhood paid about twenty-five dollars more per month than white tenants in other parts of New York City. That meant that black families often had to spend nearly half their monthly income on rent. To help make ends meet, many families threw rent parties.

The hosts of a rent party printed up colorful cards announcing the date, time, and place. On the night of the party, they moved their living room furniture and rolled back the carpet. They found chairs for the musicians, who often included a pianist, saxophone player, and drummer. The hostess set out an assortment of home-style foods, such as fried chicken, boiled pigs' feet, ham hocks, cabbage, and collard greens. Guests paid anywhere from a dime to a half-dollar for admission. They enjoyed the food and the homemade corn liquor for sale in the kitchen or hall. Most of all, they enjoyed dancing until the early morning hours, staging contests and inventing new dance steps. A successful party could earn the hosts enough money to pay the month's rent. These lively get-togethers were also a way for black people from all over Harlem to mix and mingle.

Street Shadows by the influential Harlem Renaissance artist Jacob Lawrence

Flournoy Miller *(left)* and Aubrey Lyles *(right)* perform in a 1930s revival of the groundbreaking musical *Shuffle Along*.

Bert Williams, and George Walker, had staged musical shows in New York. For most black performers, though, the only available outlet for their talents was the traveling minstrel show. This popular form of entertainment featured white singers, dancers, and comedians who blackened their faces and portrayed ignorant, happy-go-lucky "darkies." Black performers in minstrel shows had to act out the same ridiculous stereotypes. Some even put on coal black makeup to give white audiences the exaggerated, comical characters they expected.

In the early 1920s, a talented black musical team found a way for black performers to practice their craft while preserving their dignity. Singer-pianist Noble Sissle and pianist-composer Eubie Blake teamed up with songwriters Flournoy Miller and Aubrey Lyles to create a new musical comedy. *Shuffle Along* broke all the rules. Not only was the play written and produced by African Americans, but it also had an all-black cast. It even featured a serious love scene between a black man and woman—something never before seen on an American stage. When the show opened in New York in May 1921, the cast members who were not on stage during that tender scene stood near an exit, just in case outraged white theatergoers got violent. Instead, the whole audience, white and black, erupted in applause. The play was a smash hit! *Shuffle Along* became the most popular show in New York, running on Broadway for a full year before embarking on a two-year cross-country tour.

The success of *Shuffle Along* ushered in a new era for African-American performers on Broadway. Over the next two decades, New York theaters would stage at least forty black musicals. The shows made stars out of a number of talented black entertainers, including actress Florence Mills, singer Ethel Waters, and Bill "Bojangles" Robinson, often called the best tap dancer of all time.

Musical theater also helped launch the career of one of America's greatest dramatic actors and concert singers, Paul Robeson. Robeson had been educated as a lawyer, but his frustration with racism's grip on that profession led him to a stage career. He played leading roles in the Broadway play *Porgy*, the 1930 London production of William Shakespeare's *Othello*, and *The Emperor Jones*, a drama by the famous white American playwright Eugene O'Neill. His powerful performance of the song "Ol' Man River" in the musical *Show Boat* brought him international acclaim. Robeson also thrilled audiences with solo concerts of traditional black spirituals, which he called "the soul of the race made manifest."

Throughout his life Paul Robeson also spoke out against all forms of racial oppression. His passionate views brought him condemnation from the U.S. government and sometimes from conservative black leaders. But Robeson remained unbowed. "In my music, my plays, my films," he said, "I want to carry always this central idea: to be African. Multitudes of men have died for less worthy ideals; it is even more eminently worth living for."

Paul Robeson won international acclaim for his powerful performances in the stage and screen versions of *Show Boat*.

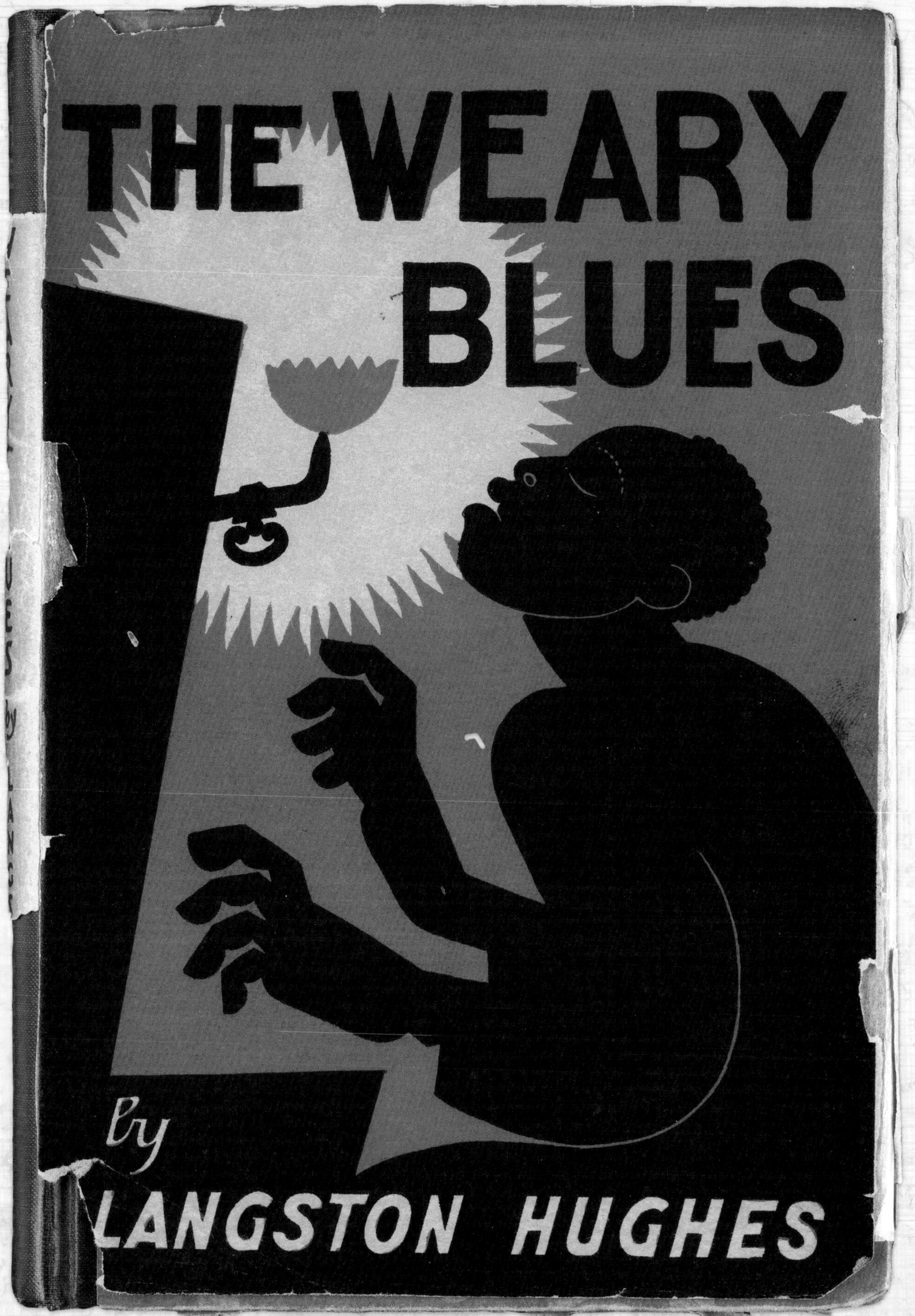
THE WEARY BLUES
By
LANGSTON HUGHES

FINDING A VOICE

THE HARLEM RENAISSANCE INVOLVED ALL THE arts. For many people, though, the flowering of writing was the "real" Renaissance. By the mid-1920s, Harlem was home to a thriving colony of young black writers, who often got together to socialize and share their thoughts and ideas. These talented people produced poetry, short stories, novels, and plays that expressed their special experiences as African Americans. The body of work they created was not only excellent in itself but also inspired future generations of black writers, who would trace their roots back to this exciting period in American literature.

SETTING THE STANDARD

Two of the leading black intellectuals of the Harlem Renaissance, W. E. B. DuBois and James Weldon Johnson, were also accomplished writers. DuBois's long literary career began in 1882, when

Opposite: Langston Hughes became the voice of black America with his first collection of poetry, *The Weary Blues.*

he published his first articles in a New York newspaper. Over the next seven decades, he would write more than twenty books, both fiction and nonfiction, along with thousands of essays, articles, and poems. All of his writings were dedicated to exposing the evils of racial prejudice and injustice and uplifting the race.

James Weldon Johnson wrote poetry, novels, nonfiction books, and songs for Broadway musicals. (You can read about his most popular song, "Lift Every Voice and Sing," on page 23.) In 1912 this multitalented black leader published *The Autobiography of an Ex-Colored Man*. The novel was praised for its vivid descriptions of ghetto life and its portrayal of one man's struggles to come to terms with what it meant to be black in America. Often called the best novel by an African American before the 1920s, the book helped pave the way for the literature of the Harlem Renaissance.

Another influential early writer was Jean Toomer. Toomer was a light-skinned black man who was often mistaken for white. As a child he had lived in two worlds. He spent his early years in a prosperous all-white neighborhood in Washington, D.C., then moved with his family to a more modest home in a black section of the city. After drifting through a series of odd jobs, he went to work for a few months at a school in the rural South. That experience changed his life. "For the first time I really saw the Negro," he told a friend, and "heard the folk-songs rolling up the valley at twilight."

Embracing his black heritage, Toomer wrote his only book, *Cane*. Published in 1923, the unusual novel combined poems, stories, plays, and literary sketches of southern life. It explored the meaning of black life in the rural South and the urban North, while tracing Toomer's restless search for his own racial identity.

STROLLING IN BLACK MANHATTAN

In 1930 James Weldon Johnson published *Black Manhattan*, a history of African Americans in New York from the earliest settlements through the Harlem Renaissance. This excerpt from Johnson's book describes one of the highlights of Harlem social life: the Sunday afternoon stroll along "Harlem's Broadway," Seventh Avenue.

One puts on one's best clothes and fares forth to pass the time pleasantly with the friends and acquaintances and, most important of all, the strangers he is sure of meeting. One saunters along, he hails this one, exchanges a word or two with that one, stops for a short chat with the other one. He comes up to a laughing, chattering group, in which he may have only one friend or acquaintance, but that gives him the privilege of joining in. He does join in and takes part in the joking, the small talk and gossip, and makes new acquaintances. . . . This is not simply going out for a walk; it is more like going out for an adventure.

Above: Three young women show off their finery during a walk along 127th Street in Harlem.

The African-American literary critic William Stanley Braithwaite called *Cane* "a book of gold and bronze, of dusk and flame, of ecstasy and pain." The experimental novel set the standard of excellence for all the up-and-coming young writers of the Harlem Renaissance.

Novelist Jean Toomer and his first wife, Margery Latimer. Toomer, who came from a racially mixed background, refused to be labeled as either black or white.

"First Fruits"

One of the guests at Charles S. Johnson's Civic Club dinner in March 1924 was Paul Kellogg. Kellogg was the editor of an influential literary magazine called *Survey Graphic*. Like the other white editors and publishers attending the dinner, he had never paid much attention to African-American culture. Now the gathering of talented young black writers had given him an idea. *Survey Graphic* would publish a special issue devoted entirely to black literature and art.

Alain Locke was asked to serve as guest editor of the "Harlem issue." The black intellectual carefully selected works by the brightest young poets, essayists, and illustrators of the time. The special issue of *Survey Graphic* appeared in March 1925. It was a huge success, selling more copies than any other issue in the magazine's history.

Later that year, Locke expanded the special magazine issue into his influential book *The New Negro*. He dedicated the anthology of black art and literature to the young black men and women who were "finding a new soul" through their "unusual outburst of creative expression." Their writings, Locke proclaimed, were "the first fruits of the Negro Renaissance. Youth speaks, and the voice of the New Negro is heard."

BLACK POETS SING

The New Negro featured nearly every one of the young black writers who would soon set the literary world ablaze. Represented in the poetry section were three of the brightest stars of the Harlem Renaissance: Langston Hughes, Claude McKay, and Countee Cullen.

Langston Hughes came to Harlem in 1921. The nineteen-year-old from Missouri had already won acclaim for his poem "The Negro Speaks of Rivers," which had been published in the NAACP journal *The Crisis.* By the time he was twenty-four, he would publish his first volume of poetry, *The Weary Blues.* The poems in that groundbreaking collection captured the spirit of black America. Hughes portrayed African Americans realistically and with dignity. He used the everyday language spoken on the streets of Harlem. He also experimented with setting his words to the rhythms of jazz and blues. In the title poem, "The Weary Blues," the narrator is listening to an old musician perform in Harlem.

> *With his ebony hands on each ivory key*
> *He made that poor piano moan with melody.*
>   *O Blues!*
> *Swaying to and fro on his rickety stool*
> *He played that sad raggy tune like a musical fool.*
>   *Sweet Blues!**

*You can read the full text of Langston Hughes's "The Weary Blues" online at
http://cai.ucdavis.edu/uccp/workingweary.html

"THE NEGRO SPEAKS OF RIVERS"

Langston Hughes wrote his first nationally recognized poem in 1920, while traveling by train to visit his father in Mexico. The seventeen-year-old had a stormy relationship with his father, a light-skinned black man who felt nothing but contempt for his own race. Dreading the meeting, Hughes stared moodily out the train window, watching the landscape change as he moved farther and farther south. At day's end the train crossed the Mississippi River. The light of the setting sun turned the deep muddy waters to gold. Pulling an envelope from his pocket, the young man began to scribble verses about life and death, hope and despair. Within a few minutes, he had written "The Negro Speaks of Rivers," a poem that rejected his father's racial hatred and embraced his proud, strong, enduring people.

I've known rivers:

I've known rivers ancient as the world and older than the
    flow of human blood in human veins.

My soul has grown deep like the rivers.

I bathed in the Euphrates when dawns were young.
I built my hut near the Congo and it lulled me to sleep.
I looked upon the Nile and raised the pyramids above it.
I heard the singing of the Mississippi when Abe Lincoln
    went down to New Orleans, and I've seen its muddy
    bosom turn all golden in the sunset.

I've known rivers:
Ancient, dusky rivers.
My soul has grown deep like the rivers.

Above left: Langston Hughes in 1924
Above right: Hughes wrote out this copy of "The Negro Speaks of Rivers."

Langston Hughes went on to publish fifteen more volumes of poetry, along with two novels, several children's books, essays, newspaper columns, plays, songs, short stories, histories, and an autobiography. He traveled to Mexico, Cuba, Haiti, France, Spain, Italy, the Soviet Union, Japan, China, and Africa. But he always returned home to Harlem, which he called "the greatest Negro city in the world."

Claude McKay also wrote poetry that explored the spirit of black life. Born and raised in Jamaica, McKay won early honors for poems written in the dialect (speech patterns) of black Jamaican country folk. In 1912 he migrated to the United States. Settling in New York, he began to write about black life in America's white-dominated society. McKay's outrage at prejudice, discrimination, and racial violence erupted in poems including "Enslaved," "In Bondage," "The Lynching," and "If We Must Die" (see page 15). He also wrote about his longing for the island life he had left behind. In his poem "When Dawn Comes to the City," McKay contrasted peaceful images of Jamaica with America's gritty urban landscape.

> *The tired cars go grumbling by,*
> *The moaning, groaning cars,*
> *And the old milk carts go rumbling by*
> *Under the same dull stars.*
> *Out of the tenements, cold as stone,*
> *Dark figures start for work;*
> *I watch them sadly shuffle on,*
> *'Tis dawn, dawn in New York.**

*You can read the full text of Claude McKay's "When Dawn Comes to the City" online at http://www.theotherpages.org/poems/mckay03.html#51

Aaron Douglas, the "Father of African-American Art," illustrated the cover of Claude McKay's *Home to Harlem.*

By 1922, Claude McKay had grown tired of "the hot syncopated fascination of Harlem [and] the suffocating ghetto of color consciousness." He escaped overseas and spent the next twelve years in Russia, Germany, France, and North Africa. Setting aside poetry, he concentrated on writing novels. Although he was far from home, his work still reflected his American roots. His novel *Home to Harlem*, published in 1928, was set amid the hustle and bustle of Harlem's streets and speakeasies. The popular book became the first best-selling novel by an African-American writer.

In contrast to the passionate writings of Langston Hughes and Claude McKay, Countee Cullen had a gentle, lyrical style. As a young man, Cullen insisted that he was "going to be POET and not NEGRO POET." At the same time, he acknowledged that racial consciousness "colors my writing, I fear, in spite of everything that I can do." Even the titles of Cullen's volumes of poetry reflected his preoccupation with racial issues: *The Ballad of the Brown Girl, Copper Sun, The Black Christ, Color.* In one of his best-known poems, "Yet Do I Marvel," he ponders the mysterious works of God and ends with these lines: "Yet do I marvel at this curious thing:/To make a poet black, and bid him sing!"

Other notable writers of the Harlem Renaissance included novelists Wallace Thurman and Walter White, poet Sterling Brown, poet and novelist Arna Bontemps, and short story writer Eric Walrond. Journalist George S. Schuyler wrote *Black No More*, the first full-length satire by an African American. This hilarious novel casts a sharp eye on racism, ignorance, and hypocrisy among both white and black Americans. It also

THE "RIGHT" WAY TO WRITE

Throughout the Harlem Renaissance, a debate raged over the question of how African Americans should be portrayed in literature, music, and art. W. E. B. DuBois and other conservative black leaders believed that art was first and foremost a tool for "race building." In their view writers and artists had a duty to present their fellow African Americans as capable, hardworking, and respectable. They hoped that this would help bring an end to prejudice and discrimination.

DuBois often criticized black writers who set their stories and poems in Harlem's nightclubs and speakeasies. He condemned the use of street slang and rural dialects. When he read Claude McKay's novel *Home to Harlem*, which includes scenes of sex, drunkenness, and fighting, he wrote, "After the dirtier part of its filth I feel distinctly like taking a bath."

Most of the younger writers and artists of the Harlem Renaissance rejected this conservative point of view. They believed in creating art for art's sake. Their works would present an honest, unfiltered view of African-American life, both the good and the bad. "We younger Negro artists who create now intend to express our individual dark-skinned selves without fear or shame," proclaimed Langston Hughes.

If white people are pleased we are glad. If they are not, it doesn't matter. We know we are beautiful. And ugly too. . . . If colored people are pleased we are glad. If they are not, their displeasure doesn't matter either. We build our temples for tomorrow, strong as we know how, and we stand on top of the mountain, free within ourselves.

Above: Sterling Brown belonged to the younger generation of poets whose writings drew on black folk traditions and rural dialects.

pokes fun at a number of African-American leaders, including Marcus Garvey (who appears as Santop Licorice) and W. E. B. DuBois (Doctor Shakespeare Agamemnon Beard).

WOMEN WRITERS OF THE RENAISSANCE

The talented writers of the Harlem Renaissance included a host of women: Zora Neale Hurston, Jessie Redmon Fauset, Nella Larsen, Anne Spencer, Gwendolyn Bennett, Georgia Douglas Johnson, Helene Johnson, Carrie Clifford, Allison Davis, and others. While they produced many different kinds of writings, most of these gifted young women were poets at heart.

The best-known female Renaissance writer was Zora Neale Hurston. Born in Florida, Hurston had worked as a maid, manicurist, and as wardrobe mistress for a traveling theatrical company before coming to Harlem in 1924. An inexhaustible writer, she turned out not only poetry but also short stories, novels, plays, and scholarly essays. Hurston often based her work on traditional black folktales, which she collected during her travels across the South, the Caribbean Islands, and Latin America. Her writings were lively and often humorous. Some black writers and intellectuals criticized her for not focusing more seriously on issues of racial conflict. Hurston answered her critics in a 1928 essay titled "How It Feels to Be Colored Me."

> I am not tragically colored. There is no great sorrow dammed up in my soul, nor lurking behind my eyes. I do not mind at all. I do not belong to the sobbing school of Negrohood who hold that nature somehow has given them a lowdown dirty deal and whose feelings are all hurt about it.
>
> Even in the helter-skelter skirmish that is my life,

I have seen that the world is to the strong regardless of a little pigmentation or less. No, I do not weep at the world—I am too busy sharpening my oyster knife."*

Poet, novelist, and folklorist Zora Neale Hurston

Jessie Redmon Fauset also aimed to rise above the tragedy of racial discrimination, while showing the world the intelligence and strength of black women. Fauset was working as a French teacher at a high school in Washington, D.C., when she began to submit poems and essays to the NAACP journal *The Crisis.* Recognizing her talent, W. E. B. DuBois asked her to come to New York. Fauset became the editor of *The Brownies' Book*, an NAACP magazine for black children. She went on to serve as literary editor of *The Crisis.* There she helped nurture the talents of many young black writers, including Langston Hughes, Claude McKay, and Countee Cullen. She also wrote romantic poetry, short stories, and four novels. Fauset's writings reflected her pride in her racial heritage. At the same time, many of her characters were upper middle-class African Americans with the same kinds of problems as well-to-do whites. In the foreword to her novel *The Chinaberry Tree*, she explained that her goal was to depict "something of the home life of the colored American who is not being pressed too hard by the Furies of Prejudice, Ignorance and Economic Injustice. And behold he is not so vastly different from any other American."

Jessie Redmon Fauset wrote about the struggles of the black middle class.

Oyster knife refers to the expression "The world is your oyster," meaning that all the good things in life—the pearl at the center of the oyster—are there for the taking. You can read the full text of Zora Neale Hurston's "How It Feels to Be Colored Me" online at http://beatl.barnard.columbia.edu/wsharpe/citylit/colored_me.htm

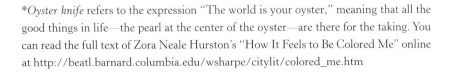

Chapter 5

THE ART OF BLACK AMERICA

BEFORE THE 1900S, MOST AMERICANS WOULD have laughed at the idea of a black person making a living from fine art. Nearly all American art schools refused to admit black students. Museums and art galleries would not display their works. Even whites who supported the struggle for civil rights often believed that African Americans should concentrate on improving their political and economic status, not on "frivolous" activities such as art.

Some artistic black people responded by applying their talents to practical crafts such as cabinetmaking and needlework. In the 1800s a handful of African-American artists, including Joshua Johnston and Robert Scott Duncanson, won recognition as portrait and landscape painters. Others moved to Europe, where they would be judged by their talent, not the color of their skin. Most notable among these was Henry Tanner. Born in

Opposite: Palmer Hayden, who created *The Janitor Who Paints* around 1937, worked as a janitor and handyman to support his artistic career.

Aaron Douglas incorporated African themes in the illustrations for this Wallace Thurman novel.

Pennsylvania in 1859, Tanner spent most of his adult life in Paris, where his paintings of religious subjects won international acclaim.

For the most part, the work of early African-American artists was similar in style and theme to that of white artists. The Harlem Renaissance changed all that. Like black musicians and writers, the visual artists of the Renaissance embraced their cultural heritage. Many black painters and sculptors began to incorporate elements of traditional African art in their work. They created art that reflected the day-to-day realities of racial injustice. They also answered three centuries of white dominance by capturing the beauty of black subjects. The work of these artists gave the world its first "inside" look at African-American life.

A SCULPTOR AWAKENS

The first African-American artist to draw deeply on African themes was Meta Warrick Fuller. Born in Philadelphia in 1877, Fuller was educated at the Pennsylvania Museum School for Industrial Arts. Traveling to Paris, she studied with the famous French sculptor Auguste Rodin. In 1903 she returned to the United States. Settling near Boston, she went to work in a studio that she built with her own hands.

Meta Fuller created sculptures inspired by her African heritage and the oppression of black people in America. Her two most famous works were *Ethiopia Awakening* (created in 1914) and *Mary Turner: A Silent Protest Against Mob Violence* (1919). *Ethiopia Awakening* is a bronze sculpture of a woman who looks very much like an ancient Egyptian funeral figure. Half bound in the restrictive wrappings of a mummy, the figure seems to be awakening from the deep sleep of the past to a future of hope, pride, and self-awareness. *Mary Turner* memorializes a pregnant black woman who was lynched in Georgia in 1917. The painted plaster sculpture shows Mary struggling to rise above racial violence and oppression.

In a narrow sense, the works of Meta Warrick Fuller do not belong to the Harlem Renaissance. She never lived in Harlem. She created much of her best work a decade before the Renaissance began. However, her sculptures captured the spirit of the emerging movement, serving as a guiding light for a new generation of black artists.

PAINTING THE SOUL

Aaron Douglas is often called the Father of African-American Art. Born in Topeka, Kansas, Douglas studied fine art at the University of Nebraska. He was teaching art at a Kansas high school when he saw the 1925 "Harlem issue" of *Survey Graphic.* Inspired by the exciting happenings in Harlem, he decided to quit his job and pursue his dream of a career in art.

Douglas arrived in Harlem short on money but loaded with talent and ambition. Two lucky encounters set the course of his future career. First, Douglas met Winold Reiss, a white German painter famous for his use of African folk characters. Reiss encouraged the young artist to move beyond his training in traditional European art and explore his African roots. Douglas also made the acquaintance of Albert Barnes, a white art patron whose collection included outstanding examples of modern European paintings and West African sculpture. Studying these masterpieces, Douglas began to develop his

Meta Warrick Fuller described *Ethiopia Awakening* as an African American "gradually unwinding the bandages of [the] past and looking out on life again, expectant and unafraid."

Winold Reiss created this inspiring view of *Dawn in Harlem* for the 1925 "Harlem issue" of *Survey Graphic*.

own unique style. His paintings combined the themes and simplicity of African art with modern elements such as cubism, in which subjects are portrayed with geometric shapes.

Aaron Douglas's groundbreaking style made him one of America's best-known artists. He created covers for several popular magazines as well as the NAACP's *Crisis*, the Urban League's *Opportunity*, and the black literary journal *Fire!!* He also painted covers and illustrations for books by many of the leading Renaissance writers and intellectuals, including James Weldon Johnson, Alain Locke, Countee Cullen, and Langston Hughes. In a letter to Hughes, Douglas shared his vision for the artists, writers, and performers of the Harlem Renaissance. "Let's bare our arms," he wrote, "and plunge them deep through laughter, through pain, through sorrow, through hope, through disappointment, into the very depths of the souls of our people and drag forth material crude, rough, neglected. Then let's sing it, dance it, write it, paint it."

Douglas completed his most famous work around the end of the Renaissance. *Aspects of Negro Life* was a series of murals created for the Harlem branch of the New York Public Library. The four monumental paintings chart the African-American experience, from freedom in Africa to slavery, emancipation, Reconstruction, and the birth of Jim Crow. In the final panel, a jazz musician stands atop a giant factory wheel, representing the New Negro's struggles for freedom and opportunity in the urban North.

NEW STYLES, NEW TRADITIONS

Other important artists of the Harlem Renaissance included painters Palmer Hayden and William H. Johnson, sculptor Augusta Savage, and photographer James Van Der Zee. Each of these artists had his or her own unique style. Together their works celebrated black history and culture and established new traditions for African-American art.

Palmer Hayden was a World War I veteran who arrived in New York in 1919. Hayden was fascinated by traditional African-American customs, legends, and folk heroes. He often incorporated these themes in vibrant Harlem street scenes and paintings of small-town life in his native Virginia. Some critics accused Hayden of encouraging stereotypes by portraying his black subjects like characters in minstrel shows. The artist answered that he simply exaggerated his subjects' appearance the way folktales embellished the speech and mannerisms of black characters.

William H. Johnson was seventeen when he went to New York to study at the National Academy of Design. The young artist launched his career with canvases painted in a traditional, realistic style. A few years later, Johnson traveled to Paris.

Wealthy art patron Albert Barnes helped launch the careers of several important Harlem Renaissance artists.

Self-Portrait by
William H. Johnson,
painted around 1934

There he immersed himself in the expressive paintings of modern European artists including Vincent van Gogh and Chaim Soutine. He began to experiment with a more "primitive" style, using simplified forms, flat two-dimensional images, and bright, contrasting colors. Johnson applied his new style to paintings of Harlem's social and political life and landscapes drawn from memories of his childhood in the South. Some critics called his style awkward and childlike. Today he is recognized for his sophisticated approach to color and for his use of small details to portray the inner strength of his subjects and the richness of African-American culture.

Augusta Savage was one of several young black sculptors who followed in Meta Warrick Fuller's footsteps. Growing up in northern Florida, Augusta showed a talent for modeling figures from the area's thick red clay. As a young woman, she entered her sculptures in a competition at a county fair, winning a top prize. That success inspired her to become a professional artist. Savage moved to New York in 1921 and soon made her name creating portrait sculptures of famous black leaders, including W. E. B. DuBois and Marcus Garvey. She also sculpted small clay statues that captured the spirit and dignity of ordinary Harlemites.

In 1929 Augusta Savage created her best-known sculpture, *Gamin.* The expressive image of a young black boy earned her a fellowship to study art in Europe. She returned to Harlem with a mission: to share her love of art with other young African Americans. Founding the Savage Studio of Arts and Crafts, she devoted her life to encouraging the next generation of black artists. Friends sometimes asked Savage why she did not spend more time on her own work. "If I can inspire one of these youngsters to develop the talent I know they possess," she replied, "then my monument will be their work. No one could ask more than that."

Augusta Savage's *Gamin* captures the spirit of a young, inquisitive, street-smart boy.

THE PERFECT PICTURE

While black painters and sculptors gave the world their personal vision of black life, James Van Der Zee captured Harlem itself. African Americans from all walks of life went to Van Der Zee's photography studio on Lenox Avenue to record special occasions such as graduations, weddings, and baptisms. The talented artist-photographer worked hard to

PATRONS OF THE ARTS

Augusta Savage supported herself cleaning houses and taking in laundry. Palmer Hayden worked as a janitor and handyman. It was often hard for the young artists and writers of the Harlem Renaissance to earn a living through creative work alone, especially early in their careers. Many relied on the helping hands of wealthy patrons. The most important art patron was William Harmon. In 1922 this white real-estate tycoon established a foundation to advance the careers of aspiring black artists. The Harmon Foundation sponsored national competitions, awards programs, and art exhibitions. Its programs helped launch the careers of Meta Fuller, Aaron Douglas, and many other artists, while introducing African-American art to a worldwide audience.

Other prominent white patrons included the wealthy widow Charlotte van der Veer Quick Mason and Carl Van Vechten, author of the controversial novel *Nigger Heaven*. Joel Spingarn; his wife, Amy; and his brother Arthur established the Spingarn Medal, which awarded annual cash prizes for outstanding achievements by African Americans.

The most important black patron of the arts was A'Lelia Walker. A'Lelia was the daughter of Madame C. J. Walker, a Harlem businesswoman whose line of homemade hair care products had made her America's first black female millionaire. The young heiress used her mother's fortune to support the work of black writers and artists. She also threw hundreds of elegant parties at her New York mansion, which she called the Dark Tower. These cultural extravaganzas brought together talented young black Harlemites and influential white editors, publishers, and business barons. At one of her parties, "the hostess of Harlem" served pigs' feet and "bathtub gin" to her white guests, while black guests feasted on caviar, pheasant, and champagne.

Above: Madame C. J. Walker, Harlem businesswoman and millionaire

show his subjects at their best. He placed them before elegant painted backgrounds. He dressed them in neat, stylish clothes and posed them in a proud and confident manner. Later he touched up any imperfections in the photos, erasing skin blemishes, straightening crooked teeth, filling in bald spots. "I tried to see that every picture was better-looking than the person," explained Van Der Zee. "I wanted to make the camera take what I thought should be there."

Outside his studio James Van Der Zee photographed the people, places, and events of Harlem. He created portraits of writers, musicians, sports stars, and religious leaders. He took pictures of shops, churches, and pool halls. He recorded the return of black soldiers from World War I, the parades of Marcus Garvey and his followers, the stylish parties at A'Lelia Walker's Dark Tower. All of his subjects, young and old, famous and unknown, received the same skillful, loving treatment. The result was a fascinating collection of images that forever preserved the style and spirit of the "New Negroes" of Harlem.

Photographer James Van Der Zee captured this glamorous image of a young nightclub dancer in 1925.

Chapter 6

The End of an Era

ON OCTOBER 29, 1929, THE STOCK MARKET collapsed, plunging the United States into the Great Depression. Banks and businesses closed, and industrial production dropped 50 percent. Six million Americans lost their jobs.

The Great Depression did not burden all Americans equally. African Americans, always the last hired and the first fired, were hit even harder than whites. By 1931, one out of every three blacks was out of work, compared to one out of four whites. Many African Americans had already been living close to the poverty line. They had little or no savings to fall back on. Millions of black families lost everything: their homes, their small farms, the means of providing food, clothing, and medicine for themselves and their children. As Langston Hughes put it, "The depression brought everybody down a peg or two. And the Negroes had but few pegs to fall."*

*For more on the Great Depression, see volume 8 in this series, *Marching toward Freedom.*

Opposite: In the midst of the Great Depression, a Harlem shoe shiner waits for customers, while an unemployed man begs for change.

The effect of the Depression on Harlem was especially devastating. A February 1930 edition of the New York *Herald Tribune* reported that there was "five times as much unemployment in Harlem as in other parts of the city." The typical family's income dropped more than 40 percent, from $1,808 in 1929 to $1,019 in 1932. Meanwhile, black migrants continued to pour into the neighborhood, allowing landlords to keep rents higher than anywhere else in Manhattan.

The hard economic times would take their toll on Harlem's vibrant culture, too. The effect was not immediate. For a few years after the Wall Street crash, the good times kept rolling. But the Great Depression, along with other factors, would gradually bring about the end of the Harlem Renaissance.

To many people, the early death of art patron A'Lelia Walker marked the end of the Harlem Renaissance.

A FAREWELL TO WRITERS

Even the wealthy felt the pinch of the Great Depression. The forty-six-year-old heiress A'Lelia Walker continued her lavish parties, but she had to mortgage (borrow money against) her Harlem mansion to pay for them. Then, in August 1931, A'Lelia died of a heart attack. The "hostess of the Renaissance" was laid to rest in a silver and bronze casket. The leading lights of New York society attended her funeral. Harlem's most distinguished minister, the Reverend Adam Clayton Powell Sr., presided over the service. A nightclub quartet sang the bittersweet show tune "I'll See You Again." A mourner read "To A'Lelia," a poem composed by Langston Hughes for the occasion. "It was a grand funeral," Hughes later recalled, "and very much like a party. . . . That was really the end of the gay times of the New Negro era in Harlem."

For many black writers, the "gay times" ended with the loss of their patrons. As fortunes faded, once-generous white patrons gave up their black writers and poets along with their cars and jewelry. Meanwhile, book and magazine sales plummeted. Publishers who had to worry about costs and potential profits were less likely to take a chance on an unknown black novelist or poet. Struggling writers who had depended on a combination of patronage, writing fees, and part-time jobs might suddenly find themselves without any income at all.

By the mid-1930s, most of the leading writers and intellectuals of the Renaissance had moved away from Harlem. Alain Locke, James Weldon Johnson, Charles S. Johnson, Countee Cullen, and others turned to teaching. Some moved to Europe. Some never published again. A handful of writers and poets, including Langston Hughes and Zora Neale Hurston, continued to make contributions to black literature. The focus of their work shifted, however. Black writers no longer concentrated mainly on racial issues. Instead, like other American writers of the Depression era, they explored broader social issues such as poverty and the struggles of the working class.

THE MUSIC FADES

Like writers, many black artists lost the financial support of their patrons during the Great Depression. The Harmon Foundation held its last awards ceremony and exhibition of African-American art in 1933. A new administration in the White House soon helped fill the void. In 1935 President Franklin D. Roosevelt established the Works Progress Administration

THE "JUICE OF HUMAN LIVING"

The Works Progress Administration provided work not only for unemployed artists but also for actors, musicians, and writers. Thousands of writers worked for the WPA's Federal Writers Project. Traveling across the country, they gathered information for state guidebooks and collected the life stories of ordinary Americans.

Among the African-American writers working for the Federal Writers Project was novelist and poet Zora Neale Hurston. In 1935 Hurston published an important collection of African-American folktales titled *Mules and Men.* Three years later, she traveled to her native Florida to record the oral histories of black country folk for the Federal Writers Project. The traditional stories and songs that she collected were published for the first time in 1999, in a book called *Go Gator and Muddy the Water.* The book includes Hurston's thoughts on why folklore differs from region to region across the United States.

> Folklore is the boiled-down juice of human living. . . . In folklore, as in everything else that people create, the world is a great big old serving platter, and all the local places are like eating plates. What-ever is on the plate comes out of the platter, but each plate has a flavor of its own because the people take the universal stuff and season it to suit themselves.

Above: Zora Neale Hurston interviews two musicians on a porch in rural Florida in the 1930s.

Dancers move to the beat of African drums in this panel from Aaron Douglas's *Aspects of Negro Life* series.

(WPA) to combat Depression-era unemployment. As part of its mission, the WPA supported the work of artists, both black and white. The agency funded major art projects in New York City, including Aaron Douglas's *Aspects of Negro Life* murals. With the help of the WPA, Harlem's African-American artists enjoyed a period of great creativity, experimenting with new techniques and styles and exploring a variety of social and political themes.

The times were harder for black musicians. Many of Harlem's big nightclubs and smaller speakeasies closed in the early 1930s, throwing hundreds of performers out of work. The Cotton Club and a few other popular nightclubs hung on, but only the wealthiest whites could afford an evening at these expensive nightspots. For a time the center of nightlife moved to the cheaper speakeasies. With most Harlemites strapped for cash, however, black and white customers no longer mingled freely in these small, dark, noisy places.

In December 1933 the repeal of Prohibition dealt the death-blow to the Harlem music scene. Sneaking a drink of bootleg liquor had always been part of the attraction at the nightclubs and speakeasies. Now that alcohol was legal, white New Yorkers turned to the downtown nightclubs where big bands were playing a popular new form of jazz called swing. As black musicians and singers moved on in search of new opportunities, the gaiety of Harlem's streets gave way to a growing sense of despair.

"A DREAM DEFERRED"

By the mid-1930s, Harlem had become a dreary and desperate place. Residents struggled with unemployment, poverty, overcrowding, disease, and the inflated rents in run-down apartment buildings. Many Harlemites deeply resented the white apartment and business owners who continued to profit in their midst. On the evening of March 19, 1935, those resentments spilled over in violence.

The trouble started when a sixteen-year-old Puerto Rican boy was accused of shoplifting a ten-cent pocketknife in a white-owned department store. A white salesclerk threatened the teenager and tossed him out on the street. A rumor spread that the boy had been beaten to death. Harlem exploded in a night of rioting, with an estimated 10,000 to 20,000 angry blacks looting and burning white-owned property. By the next morning, three rioters were dead, thirty were injured, and two million dollars' worth of property had been destroyed. A Langston Hughes poem captured the feelings of rage and frustration that had led to the violence in Harlem.

What happens to a dream deferred?

Does it dry up
like a raisin in the sun
Or fester like a sore—
And then run?

. . .

Or does it explode?*

After the 1935 riot, most whites stopped going to Harlem. The Cotton Club closed its doors, along with nearly all the rest of the neighborhood's entertainment industry. Harlem's time as a special place at the center of black culture, art, and literature had come to an end.

In the years that followed, some critics argued that the impact of the Harlem Renaissance was limited, reaching a privileged few and leaving the day-to-day lives of most African Americans unaffected. In their view, white interest in black culture was just a passing fad. When white Americans moved on to the next "in thing," prejudice and discrimination continued as always.

Even the skeptics, however, acknowledged that the movement left a strong foundation for talented young African Americans to build on. The doors had been opened for young black writers, poets, artists, and musicians. The stage had been set for further explorations of black identity and the black experience. Future generations could look back with pride to a time when African Americans expressed themselves creatively and the whole world took notice.

*You can read the full text of Langston Hughes's "Dream Deferred" online at www.math.buffalo.edu/~sww/poetry/hughes_langston.html

THE RENAISSANCE REACHES AFRICA

The influence of the Harlem Renaissance reached beyond the United States, touching blacks as far away as the Caribbean Islands, South America, Europe, and Africa. Peter Abrahams was a young black man living in South Africa under the system of racial segregation known as apartheid when his life was changed by the Renaissance. In the 1930s Abrahams came across a copy of W. E. B. DuBois's book *The Souls of Black Folk.* "I turned the pages," he recalled.

It spoke about a people in a valley. And they were black, and dispossessed, and denied. . . . Du Bois had given me a key to the understanding of my world. The Negro is not free. . . . I replaced the book and reached for others. . . . I turned the pages of [Alain Locke's] *The New Negro.* These poems and stories were written by Negroes! Something burst deep inside me. The world could never again belong to white people only! Never again!

Peter Abrahams went on to become one of his country's most prominent writers. His novels were the first to document the damaging effects of racism and apartheid on blacks in South Africa. Years later, he would thank the writers of the Harlem Renaissance for "crystallizing my vague yearnings to write and for showing me the long dream was attainable."

Above: Peter Abrahams wrote the first novels about South Africa's brutal system of apartheid.

Glossary

accommodation the act of compromising with, or adapting to, an opposing point of view. *Accommodationism* often refers to the policy in which blacks adapted to the attitudes and expectations of whites.

bootleg liquor a slang term for liquor that is produced and sold illegally

dialect a regional variation of a language, which has its own unique accent, vocabulary, and grammar

emancipation freeing someone from the control or power of another

Jim Crow laws and practices designed to segregate African Americans, stripping them of their political and civil rights. The Jim Crow system arose in the South following the end of Reconstruction in 1877 and continued to the Civil Rights movement of the 1950s and 1960s.

lynch mobs lawless mobs that seize and kill people accused of offenses. Most African Americans lynched by white mobs were hanged or shot.

pan-Africanism a political movement based on the idea that people of African descent all over the world share the same history and culture and should work together to overcome common problems such as slavery, colonial oppression, and racism

ragtime an American music form that reached its height of popularity between 1890 and the late 1910s. Ragtime featured "ragged," or syncopated, rhythms and was often played on the piano.

Renaissance revival or rebirth; a period of intense intellectual and cultural activity

satire a literary work that uses ridicule and humor to expose society's flaws

segregation the practice of separating one race from another by setting up separate housing, schools, and public facilities and through other forms of discrimination

stereotypes exaggerated, usually negative images of people from a particular ethnic group, region, or religion

syncopation a type of rhythm that puts the accents off the regular beats

To Find Out More

BOOKS

Candaele, Kerry. *Bound for Glory, 1910–1930: From the Great Migration to the Harlem Renaissance.* Philadelphia: Chelsea House, 1997.

Giovanni, Nikki. *Shimmy Shimmy Shimmy Like My Sister Kate: Looking at the Harlem Renaissance through Poems.* New York: Henry Holt, 1996.

Grossman, James R. *A Chance to Make Good: African Americans 1900–1929.* New York: Oxford University Press, 1997.

Hardy, P. Stephen, and Sheila Jackson Hardy. *Extraordinary People of the Harlem Renaissance.* Danbury, CT: Children's Press, 2000.

Haskins, Jim. *The Harlem Renaissance.* Brookfield, CT: Millbrook Press, 1996.

Haskins, Jim, Eleanora Tate, Clinton Cox, and Brenda Wilkinson. *Black Stars of the Harlem Renaissance.* New York: John Wiley, 2002.

Haugen, Brenda. *Langston Hughes: The Voice of Harlem.* Minneapolis, MN: Compass Point Books, 2006.

Hill, Laban Carrick. *Harlem Stomp! A Cultural History of the Harlem Renaissance.* New York: Little Brown, 2003.

Howes, Kelly King. *Harlem Renaissance.* Detroit, MI: UXL/Gale Group, 2001.

Hughes, Langston. *The Big Sea.* New York: Hill and Wang, 1993.

McConnell, William S., ed. *Harlem Renaissance.* San Diego: Greenhaven Press, 2003.

WEB SITES

African American Odyssey: The Harlem Renaissance and the Flowering of Creativity. Library of Congress.
http://lcweb2.loc.gov/ammem/aaohtml/exhibit/aopart7b.html

Big Apple History, Arts and Entertainment: The Harlem Renaissance. PBS Kids, Educational Broadcasting Corporation.
http://pbskids.org/bigapplehistory/arts/topic9.html

Harlem 1900–1940: An African-American Community. Schomburg Center for Research in Black Culture, New York Public Library.
http://www.si.umich.edu/chico/Harlem

The Harlem Renaissance. Father Ryan High School, Nashville, Tennessee.

http://www.fatherryan.org/harlemrenaissance

In Motion, The African-American Migration Experience: The Great Migration. Schomburg Center for Research in Black Culture, New York Public Library.
http://www.inmotionaame.org/migrations/landing.cfm?migration=8

Jazz. PBS Kids, Educational Broadcasting Corporation.
http://pbskids.org/jazz/index.html

Rhapsodies in Black: Art of the Harlem Renaissance. Institute of International Visual Arts and the Hayward Gallery.
http://www.iniva.org/harlem/home.html

Selected Bibliography

Anderson, Jervis. *This Was Harlem.* New York: Farrar Straus Giroux, 1982.

Bloom, Harold, ed. *Black American Prose Writers of the Harlem Renaissance.* Philadelphia: Chelsea House, 1994.

———. *The Harlem Renaissance.* Philadelphia: Chelsea House, 2004.

Driskell, David, David Levering Lewis, and Deborah Willis Ryan. *Harlem Renaissance: Art of Black America.* New York: Studio Museum in Harlem and Harry N. Abrams, 1987.

Floyd, Samuel A. Jr., ed. *Black Music in the Harlem Renaissance.* New York: Greenwood Press, 1990.

Franklin, John Hope, and Alfred A. Moss Jr. *From Slavery to Freedom: A History of African Americans.* New York: Alfred A. Knopf, 2000.

Kramer, Victor A., and Robert A. Russ, eds. *Harlem Renaissance Reexamined.* Troy, NY: Whitson Publishing, 1997.

Lawrence, A. H. *Duke Ellington and His World.* New York: Routledge, 2001.

Lewis, David Levering, ed. *The Portable Harlem Renaissance Reader.* New York: Viking, 1994.

———. *When Harlem Was in Vogue.* New York: Penguin, 1997.

Locke, Alain, ed. *The New Negro: Voices of the Harlem Renaissance.* New York: Atheneum, 1992.

Meltzer, Milton. *The Black Americans: A History in Their Own Words, 1619–1983.* New York: HarperTrophy, 1984.

Rampersad, Arnold, ed. *The Collected Poems of Langston Hughes.* New York: Alfred A. Knopf, 1998.

Watson, Steven. *The Harlem Renaissance.* New York: Pantheon Books, 1995.

Wesley, Charles H. *The Quest for Equality: From Civil War to Civil Rights.* Cornwells Heights, PA: Publishers Agency, 1978.

Wintz, Cary D. *Black Culture and the Harlem Renaissance.* Houston, TX: Rice University Press, 1988.

Notes on Quotes

Chapter 1: Roots of the Harlem Renaissance

p. 12, "For the final mile": Lewis, *When Harlem Was in Vogue*, p. 5.

p. 14, "GIVE US A CHANCE": ibid, p. 10, and http://www.si.umich.edu/CHICO/Harlem/text/silentprotest.html

p. 14, "We return": W. E. B. DuBois, "Returning Soldiers," *The Crisis*, May 1919, in Lewis, *The Portable Harlem Renaissance Reader*, p. 5.

p. 15, "If we must die": Claude McKay, "If We Must Die," in Lewis, *The Portable Harlem Renaissance Reader*, p. 290.

p. 16, "the good old South" and "mister every little": *The Journal of Negro History*, vol. 4, 1919, at http://www.historymatters.gmu.edu/d/5339

pp. 17–18, "was moving up the coast": "Interview of Jacob Lawrence" at http://www.inmotionaame.org/migrations/topic.cfm?migration=8&topic=4

p. 18, "Negro invasion" and "wake up": Anderson, *This Was Harlem*, p. 53.

p. 19, "a Negro city": Haskins, *The Harlem Renaissance*, p. 24.

Chapter 2: A New Identity

p. 22, "renaissance of American Negro": W. E. B. DuBois, "Negro Writers," *The Crisis*, April 1920, in Watson, *The Harlem Renaissance*, p. 19.

p. 23, "Lift ev'ry voice": James Weldon Johnson, "Lift Every Voice and Sing," at http://www.poets.org/viewmedia.php/prmMID/15588

p. 24, "The world does not": James Weldon Johnson, *Writings* (New York: Library of America, 2004), p. 688.

p. 24, "spiritual Coming of Age": Alain Locke, *The New Negro*, p. 16.

p. 25, "pulse of the Negro": ibid, p. 14.

pp. 25–26, "coming out party" and "It was a most": Arna Bontemps, ed., *The Harlem Renaissance Remembered* (New York: Dodd, Mead,

1972), p. 11.

p. 26, "a little sawed-off": Lewis, *When Harlem Was in Vogue*, pp. 34–35.

p. 27, "the Negro must engage": A. Philip Randolph, *The Messenger*, July 1919, at http://www.spartacus.schoolnet.co.uk/USArandolph.htm

p. 28, "Up you mighty race": Franklin and Moss, *From Slavery to Freedom*, p. 395.

p. 28, "thousands of Garvey legionnaires": Grossman, *A Chance to Make Good*, p. 144.

p. 29, "without doubt": W. E. B. DuBois, *Writings* (New York: Library of America, 1986), p. 990.

p. 29, "Every time you see": "Marcus Garvey: The Forgotten Giant of Black Liberation" at http://www.ritesofpassage.org/m_garvey.htm

Chapter 3: The Music of the Renaissance

p. 34, "not softened with tears": Gates, Henry Louis Jr., and Cornel West, *The African American Century* (New York: Free Press, 2000), p. 111.

p. 35, "All I do is write": Lawrence, *Duke Ellington and His World*, p. 199.

p. 36, "the one place": Watson, *The Harlem Renaissance*, p. 124.

p. 37, "Harlem Negroes did not": Hughes, *The Big Sea*, pp. 224–225.

p. 38, "The average musician": Lawrence, *Duke Ellington and His World*, p. 37.

p. 41, "the soul of the race": Sterling Stuckey, *Going through the Storm: The Influence of African-American Art in History* (New York: Oxford University Press, 1994), p. 191.

p. 41, "In my music": ibid, p. 187.

Chapter 4: Finding a Voice

p. 44, "For the first time": Wintz, *Black Culture and the Harlem Renaissance*, p. 77.

p. 45, "One puts on one's": James Weldon Johnson, *Black Manhattan* (New York: Arno Press and the *New York Times*, 1968), pp. 162–163.

p. 46, "a book of gold": Wintz, *Black Culture and the Harlem Renaissance*, p. 79.

p. 46, "finding a new soul": Locke, *The New Negro*, p. xxvii.

p. 47, "the first fruits": ibid, p. 47.

p. 47, "With his ebony hands": Langston Hughes, "The Weary Blues,"

in Rampersad, *The Collected Poems of Langston Hughes*, p. 50.

p. 48, "I've known rivers": Langston Hughes, "The Negro Speaks of Rivers," in Rampersad, *The Collected Poems of Langston Hughes*, p. 23.

p. 49, "the greatest Negro city": Hughes, *The Big Sea*, p. 62.

p. 49, "The tired cars": Claude McKay, "When Dawn Comes to the City," at http://www.theotherpages.org/poems/mckay03.html#51

p. 50, "the hot syncopated fascination": Lewis, *When Harlem Was in Vogue*, p. 56.

p. 50, "going to be POET": Watson, *The Harlem Renaissance*, p. 78.

p. 50, "colors my writing": Lewis, *When Harlem Was in Vogue*, p. 77.

p. 50, "Yet do I marvel": Watson, *The Harlem Renaissance*, p. 79.

p. 51, "After the dirtier parts": Bloom, *Black American Prose Writers of the Harlem Renaissance*, p. 109.

p. 51, "We younger Negro artists": Langston Hughes, "The Negro Artist and the Racial Mountain," in McConnell, *Harlem Renaissance*, p. 173.

p. 52, "I am not tragically": Zora Neale Hurston, "How It Feels to Be Colored Me," in Watson, *The Harlem Renaissance*, p. 69.

p. 53, "something of the home": Fauset, Jessie Redmon, *The Chinaberry Tree: A Novel of American Life* (New York: G. K. Hall, 1995), p. ix.

Chapter 5: The Art of Black America

p. 58, "Let's bare our arms": Aaron Douglas to Langston Hughes, December 21, 1925, in Amy Helen Kirschke, *Aaron Douglas: Art, Race, and the Harlem Renaissance* (Jackson, MS: University Press of Mississippi, 1995), pp. 78–79.

p. 61, "If I can inspire": Haskins, *The Harlem Renaissance*, p. 159.

p. 63, "I tried to see": Haskins and others, *Black Stars of the Harlem Renaissance*, p. 46.

Chapter 6: The End of an Era

p. 65, "The depression brought everybody": Hughes, *The Big Sea*, p. 247.

p. 66, "five times as much": Hill, *Harlem Stomp!*, p. 129.

p. 66, "It was a grand": Hughes, *The Big Sea*, pp. 246–247.

p. 68, "Folklore is the boiled-down": Zora Neale Hurston, *Go Gator and Muddy the Water* (New York: W. W. Norton, 1999), p. 69.

p. 71, "What happens to a dream": Langston Hughes, "Harlem," in

Rampersad, *The Collected Poems of Langston Hughes*, p. 426.

p. 72, "I turned the pages": Peter Abrahams, *Tell Freedom: Memories of Africa* (New York: Alfred A. Knopf, 1954), pp. 224–226.

p. 72, "crystallizing my vague yearnings": ibid, p. 230.

Index